The Inspired You

Sometimes It Just Has To Be About You

BY: KENNY WHITTINGTON

SELF HELP AWARENESS

In the process of strengthening and restoration there must be space in our lives for self-help. Turning the mirror on ourselves is a way of examining the persons we have come to be. There comes a time in our lives that we take inventory of what we have done and where we have been so that we know where we are going. We might not like the results but in order to get where we need to be in Christ Jesus this can serve as our best and most effective plan. There will be times when we need to reshape our thoughts and our surroundings. The removing of unnecessary baggage whether it be people, places, or things may sometimes be the case.

Our lives are affected by many adverse situations. Our resolve as well as our integrity is tried time and time again. But through it all, it is our faith in God that becomes our strongest guiding force. It is important for us to realize that no one travels this journey alone and we can always trust and depend on God to keep us and sustain us along the way. The Word tells us that 'He knows the path we take' and so we must concede that He knows what is best for us. So, for us to reach our destination in Christ Jesus there maybe questions we need to ask ourselves.

1   ARE WE LIVING OUR BEST LIVES?
2   ARE WE BEING TRUE TO OURSELVES?
3   ARE WE GIVING GOD OUR ALL AND ALL?
4   HOW CAN I BE THE BEST PERSON I CAN BE CHRIST JESUS?

It is said that we live our lives as a tale that is untold each day being a new journey within itself. Through our journey we learn, and we evolve. We grow when we take the time and effort to place value on the things that mean the most. Live and find peace, love and find joy.

A HELPING YOU

Perhaps one of the strongest and most impactful ministries is the ministry of help. To lend aid and comfort whether be man or beast is the greatest gift of ourselves we can give. It is that special person that is able to give of his time, talent, and treasure to help change the course of another's life or be the impact we were meant to be.

Now I know that the purpose of this book is to improve who we are but what other way can we improve ourselves but through helping others. Taking time to take our minds off ourselves can help us get a better focus on the best things of life. It teaches us to appreciate what God has already done for us. It also helps us to realize that things are not as bad as we think they are.

The term "Angels of Mercy" is befitting to those who selflessly goes beyond the call of duty and lends a helping hand to those that are without or in need. The beauty of these people is that no one ever has to ask them to do, they just do. To help someone takes heart and compassion and its reward can be self-healing and fulfillment. To give hope to the hopeless, courage to the fearful, and love to the lost is a gift that keeps on giving.

Galatians 5:13   for, brethren, ye have been called unto liberty; only use not liberty for an occasion to the flesh, but by love serve one another.

ENJOYING THE BEST YOU

Our best days are yet ahead of us. In Christ Jesus, every day is sweeter than the day before because we appreciate the life that we are living and anticipating that it will be better with each day to come. With our mindset on doing better things, we have hope, love, joy, and peace. We may not have everything we want but we have just what we need to go forth. Enjoy the moment! Enjoy the time! Enjoy your family! But most of all enjoy yourself!

Contentment brings about serenity. Serenity brings a peaceful focus.

Always seek to do things better because within us there is excellence.

And so, I ask.

What is it that you would like to do? Sailing, travel, sing, write. Do it!

Where would you like to go? Then go!

What would you like to eat? Have at it! (In moderation please)

We have but one time on this earth and I wish could have, I should have or if I could have is no way to live it. No better time to enjoy this life than now.

Healing our mindset heals and frees our spirit as well as our body. Find and enjoy the things that brings out the best in you.

John 10:10 The thief cometh not, but for to steal, and to kill, and to destroy I am come that they might have life, and that they might have it more abundantly.

THE INSPIRED YOU

Our source of inspiration may come from a variety of directions. Whether it be from loved ones or something we might have read or experienced. Or through our hopes and our dreams. Maybe a sermon or a scripture or even a song. What works for some may not work for you. But there is one thing that is important to understand. An inspired you is a motivated you and a motivated you is a productive you. So, what is it that gets your juices pumping? What does it take to get your fires burning?

An inspired you creates life on many levels whether you write a novel, paint a masterpiece, love on your family or sing a song the inspired you is a source of joy. Within the inspired you is a treasure of magnificent proportions.

In this life we will face many deterrents and obstacles but, in the end, it is how we overcome them that will measure who we are. For some the greater the test the stronger they become. While others may have fallen by the wayside there is that extra something inside of you that says I must go on. I cannot and I will not stop. Determined to be the best that they can be they strive for higher heights and deeper depths in all they do. So again, I ask what is it that gets your juices pumping? What does it take to get your fires burning?

Philippians 4:13 I can do all things through Christ which strengthenth me

A GRATEFUL YOU

In all things give thanks. For life is a gift worth living and enjoying. Every breath that we take and each step we make is a blessing of its own. Wisdom and life experiences tells us that things could always be worse than they are, but we are blessed, nonetheless. Thank God for the little things and He will make room for the greater. With each experience whether bad or good we take something out of it and hopefully it will make us better than we were before.

With gratitude comes appreciation. With appreciation comes contentment. When we learn to live within ourselves, we grow day by day, step by step. A grateful you will lead to a loving heart that shares love, joy, hope, and is filled with peace. A grateful you will become an inspired you.

Psalm 106:1 Praise ye the Lord. O give thanks unto the Lord; for He is good; for His mercy endureth forever.

A DETERMINED YOU

Our mindset sets the stage for our direction and progress. If we are not wholeheartedly focused on being the best that we can be then we have opened ourselves to certain failures and pitfalls. Life by itself has a way of throwing roadblocks and distractions that cause us to detour or alter ways. But when we remain steadfast and undeterred no matter the situation good things are bound to come our way.

The Word of God holds true that a doubleminded man is unstable in all his ways. His path becomes as quicksand, unstable and full of uncertainty. When your thoughts are scattered there is no way to have full grasp of anything that goes on around you.

A determined you is a fighter that never gives up or never gives in. They keep their eyes and trust on God no matter the storm they face. For it is through that unmovable spirit that they continue to press toward the mark. It is through that determined heart that they can say that I can do all things through Christ that strengthens me.

1 Corinthians 15:58 Be ye steadfast, unmovable, always abounding in the work of the Lord for your labor is not in vain.

A CONFIDENT YOU

Trusting in what God has given and put in you to be successful takes a concerted effort. But it is that effort that is its own reward. With no room for doubt a self-assured person reaches for the stars because the skies have no limit. If one door does not open seek for another door, another way. A confident you can lead to productive and positive life. For you, no challenge is too great because your focus is razor sharp.

A confident you is a bold you. A confident you is a strong you, ever courageous because he is backed by the love of God. Ever standing on the promises of God failure is not an option. You anticipate great things because you are a child of the King. You are blessed and highly favored and nothing can stand in your way. Stand strong. Be diligent. Trust God.

Psalm 18:2 The Lord is my rock, and my fortress, and my deliverer, my God, my strength, in whom I trust.

A GODLY FOCUS

In God we have our all and all. He is the ultimate supplier of our needs both spiritually and naturally. He is our refuge from the storm, our bridge over troubled waters. He promises never to leave us nor forsake us therefore He is always with us. Our thoughts are always upon Him for He promises to keep us in perfect peace if our hearts are stayed on Him. In His Word, there are many promises that He has given to keep and sustain us through life's ups and downs. It is through His Word we find peace and joy. And with each promise fulfilled our hearts are fixed and our minds regulated to stand strong in Christ Jesus.

Our healing is in His hands because we put our trust in Him unwaveringly. It is our faith that keeps us going day by day even in our weakest moments. When we keep our focus on God, we are assured a victorious and blessed life. In Romans 8:37 we are told in all these things we are more than conquerors through him that loved us. So, in all things it behooves us to keep our focus and our hearts on Christ Jesus.

Matthew 6:33 But seek ye first the kingdom of God and his righteousness, and all these things shall be added unto you.

BE A FRIEND

Nobody travels this journey alone. Every now and then we need someone to talk to, listen to, or even touch. A friend is a gift from God that tells you that you are not alone. Whether near or far they stand with you in the best of times and encourages you through the worst of times. A friend even tells you when you are right or wrong. The bible says 'a friend loveth at all times', and surely time nor space will ever limit its strength.

Truly true friends come in short supply, and they are a treasure to be revered. Our thoughts should be that we be the kind of friend to someone that we would like them to be to us. Whether a shoulder to lean on or ear to listen be that friend that someone can count on.

Proverbs18:24 A man that hath friends must shew himself friendly: and there is a friend that sticketh closer than a brother.

STANDING STRONG

I do not look like what I have been through

I stand by faith and trust in God

The way may not be easy, but I am on my way

For the road to recovery is in Christ Jesus

Stand on His Word and trust in His way

Though the storms may rage, and the billows may roll

In Him, there is a solid foundation

My heart finds strength and courage from those who love me

Always praying yet always pushing

My eyes are ever on the Prize

For God has been good to me, so I dare not faint

Standing strong, I am on my way

   'cause I know the best is yet to come

THE EVOLVING YOU

Change is the inevitable part of life that remains constant. Whether slow or rapid it is a process that has its own course. From the time of conception, we are being molded and shaped into the person we are going to be. Each person's timeline has a different trajectory from the next. Therefore, we are likened to the caterpillar awaiting the awesome transformation of becoming that beautiful butterfly waiting to spread its wings.

O that beautiful purposeful, positive, and productive butterfly. Changing the world with the glorious marvel it has within. Blessed and favored of God your life is a gift and a joy to others. Truly guided and lead by God. Ever standing on His Word.

Our growth is an enduring process and time is our gift.

So, as we evolve, we pray we grow stronger, smarter, and wiser.

Psalm 139:14 I will praise thee: for I am fearfully and wonderfully made: marvelous are thy works, and that my soul knoweth right well.

A PRODUCTIVE YOU

Idle hands burden the heart and mind while productive hands strengthen the spirit. Looking forward to better things in ourselves become the main source of our healing. We do not want to settle for the also-ran or the mediocre. But our goal is to be the best version of ourselves that we can be. We strive to put our hands to the plow that we may reach higher heights and deeper depths in all that we are involved in.

A productive you make everything and everyone around you better. A productive you then become a satisfied you. A satisfied you is a healthy you. There is no doubt that when a person is productive, they become a viable force creating positivity everywhere they go. Productive people inspire and replicate others to be like them.

There is much to be done in this lifetime. Whatever we can put our hands to do we should do with vigor and commitment. For surely life is too short to lay back dreaming of what could have or what should have been.

Proverbs 18:9 He also that is slothful in his work is brother to him that is a great waster.

John 9:4 I must work the works of him that sent me, while it is day: the night cometh, when no man can work.

A POSITIVE YOU

Success in all things start in our minds. We must see it to achieve it. We must feel it to believe it. To go forward we need to see ourselves already there. It is true that we are faced with many challenges and life changing circumstances, but do we allow it to define us, or do we make the best of what has been. If we fall, we can get up. If we stumble, we do not have to stop. With each step we take our eyes should be looking to go further and higher than ever before. Our desire should be to be a blessing to others as God has blessed us.

Ever trusting God for the path that He has placed us on with every step we take we choose not to let anything hinder our way. For we are always reaching for the better yet seeking for the best. A positive you find strength and resilience from within and does not allow himself to settle for less than the best.

With no holds barred by faith we trust in God for our beginning and our end. His Word is a light unto path, and we are blessed in all our ways. So let our thoughts remain heaven bound for God's children deserve the best for (Romans 8:37) says 'we are more than conquerors through him that loved us'. I am strong. I am healed. I am wonderful. I am not alone. But most of all I am blessed.

Phil 2:5 Let this mind be in you, which was also in Christ Jesus.

A GIVING YOU

A giving heart is a loving heart. A loving heart is a godly heart. Our time, our talent, and our treasure are "The All" that we have to give, and we should give it wholeheartedly. And for the child of God, it is done with soulful contentment. To give of oneself is a selfless act that does not always receive or seek accolades. Just to see a need and be a part can be its own reward. To make a difference and help renew hope is a blessed gift that keeps on giving.

A giving heart shall lack for naught. For it heals and comforts therefore peace is always within its grasp. It seeks not its own but is fulfilled within its being. A better you is a better me. To God be the glory.

The giving of yourself can fill the emptiness of others as well as yourself.

Matt. 5:7 Blessed are the merciful, for they shall obtain mercy.

8 Blessed are the pure in heart, for they shall see God.

THINKING OUT OF THE BOX

Maybe it is time to get out of our comfort zones. If we are not careful, we can run into a mundane routine that can keep us stagnate and fruitless. Life is for the living so why not live it to its fullest. We only hinder ourselves when we cannot see pass today or live without faith. If you can dream it why not do it. With all that we do we should seek to do things better. In this life we are called to face challenge after challenge, test after test but with each we should find some sort of growth or improvement. What may seem impossible will remain impossible if we limit the way we think and handle what is at hand. Reach for that higher height, seek that deeper depth. Reach beyond your fingertips and grab a star. There are still wonders to enjoy and treasures to be found.

Time out for the' woe is me syndrome'. Our faith in God will take us where some dare not go and others can only dream. Trusting God opens doors and paths we cannot see with our eyes. It takes us beyond ourselves and is a fulltime commitment and step by step journey. We have been created to do great and awesome things but none of these will occur if we are stuck in our box confined in the shallow walls of our minds. So go forth.

Phil.4:13 I can do all things through Christ which strengthenth me.

A SELFISH YOU

Think of all the adages you have learned and the quotes that you have heard. Now put a pin in it. Wisdom teaches us to respect each angle. It teaches us to find value in the conclusion of the matter. So let us understand that taking time for you may be the healthiest thing you can do. Even Jesus needed some time alone to regain His virtue. Matt 26:36

We give because we love, we love because we give. But sometimes we give all that we have and that from time to time needs to be restored. It is important for us to enjoy the fruits of life and the labor in which it took to get there. A little rest, a little love, a time to laugh, and a time to enjoy. Each has its place in our lives. We are no good to others if we are broken and no good for ourselves. The joy of life and the peace in our spirit is our greatest assets. Cherish it, nurture it, and it will keep you.

Ecc. 3: 12 I know that there is no good in them, but for a man to rejoice, and to do good in his life.

13 And also that every man should eat and drink, and enjoy the good of all his labour, it is the gift of God.

A CARING HEART

A heart of love that gives hope and compassion to the weary and the lost

It reaches above and beyond

Strengthening the feeble and mending the brokenhearted

Ever giving hope to the hopeless

The caring heart gives of itself when there is nothing else to give

Bringing warmth and life

It is array of hope that brings light to the darkened path

A refuge for the tattered soul

The caring heart is an angel of mercy

A renewing of strength, a restorer of joy

It is a gift from God

A treasure more precious than silver or gold

AN ACCEPTING YOU

With each journey or battle that we face understanding what is before us can make all the difference in the world. Some obstacles may be harder than others. Some deficits may be greater than others. But realize that each thing that we go through it comes to make us strong and has a purpose for being. And though we may not understand why they are upon us, trusting God helps us to bear a little longer.

We accept that it is through Him that all things are done therefore allowing us to put our faith in Him. We put our trust in Him because He is making us and molding us to be the men and women, He is calling us to be. We stumble when we resist the journey and lose our way. But when we accept the path that He has put us on the way becomes a little lighter because He knows what is best for us.

Proverbs 3:5 Trust in the Lord with all thine heart; and lean not unto thine own understanding.

6 in all thy ways acknowledge him, and he shall direct thy paths.

AN INSIGHTFUL YOU

For the child of God having a clear and deep understanding of their purpose in Christ Jesus is invaluable. We walk by faith and not by sight is true but when we understand our purpose the direction that we take becomes clearer and fuller of meaning. God has a plan for us and for us is to trust the way.

The insightful you follow Christ without doubt or apprehension. They follow the leading of the Lord despite the roadblocks and distractions that come along the way because they know He is a way maker. As they follow the Word of God, they can apply the Word to their lives daily and find what they need to go forth. The insightful person know it is the wisdom of the Word that all things work for the good of them who are called to His purpose.

The insightful you relies on the joy of the Lord to be their strength and their keeper.

Isaiah 26:3 Thou will keep him in perfect peace, whose mind is stayed on thee because he trusteth in thee.

STAYING SMART (STAYING WITHIN YOURSELF)

There is a fine line between faith and fool heartiness. Wise counsel comes from many sources which may include our doctors or our loved ones. In the chapters past we spoke of thinking out of the box or thinking beyond our normal. But remember with every action there is a reaction, and every action has a price. Count the cost, do your due diligence. For surely haste make waste.

Nothing more powerful can mess up your reconstruction than an ill-advised action. These things can include a poor diet, little rest, poor company, and hardheadedness. Hint: Isn't that what brought us here initially?

Patience is a virtue and time is a gift that we need to cherish.

If you don't know, pray.

Stay safe. Stay strong. Stay blessed.

Romans 8:28 And we know that all things work together for good to them that love God, to them who are the called according to his purpose.

QUIPS AND QUOTATIONS

Stay safe. Stay strong stay blessed.

Trust God

Always have a plan.

Slow down.

Be productive,

Be positive

Live your dream, Don't dream your life

Stay effective and be efficient

Push,Push,Push

A PRAYERFUL YOU

It is a faithful saying that goes 'prayer is the key, but our faith unlocks the door'. A prayerful person is a powerful person because he knows in whom his strength lies. A prayerful you know that God is our provider as well as our keeper. It is their relationship with God that keeps them steadfast and strong. Even in the midst of adversity he knows he must stand still and see the salvation of God. They patiently wait on God for He knows the best path for us.

A prayerful you seek godly direction and trust God's judgement for the journey He has placed him. His relationship with God hinges on his ability to communicate constantly with the Father. It is an unwavering prayer life that centers all that he does as he seeks favor from God. He knows God is his joy and his strength, so he dares not risk anything from separating him. A true prayer warrior knows that a humble and thankful heart is the path to pleasing God. It is when we pray, we say that trust God and depend on him. It is when we pray, we surrender unto His will and His way.

James 5:16 The effectual fervent prayer of a righteous man availeth much.

A SIMPLE THOUGHT

Just a simple thought to brighten your day

A simple smile to lighten your load

Just a simple thought to bring you hope

A simple grin to spread some joy

Think on things that encourage your heart

Lean on things that make you strong

Bless those who are afar

And love on those who are ever so near

A gracious heart yields a humble spirit

A humble spirit creates a peaceful soul

And a peaceful soul enlightens hope for all

Just a simple thought to brighten your day

KNOWING YOURSELF

With each journey, project or task that we will face there must be a beginning. A ground zero to measure where we have been so that we know where we are going. It helps launches us into bigger and better things if we know where we came from. Knowing ourselves gives us the blueprint into becoming the best versions ourselves that we can be. We need to know our strengths as well as our weaknesses. We need to know what makes us happy as well as what drives us off key.

In knowing yourself you are able to be true to yourself. When we are taken out of character, we lose the most important part of ourselves which is our self-esteem. Our self-esteem whether high or low impacts the quality of person we are meant to be. It is that self-esteem that gives us value and self-worth and as children of the King we deserve to live the best lives we can live.

When we are in-tuned with ourselves we are God's greatest creation blessed and highly favored. We are holy treasures endowed with the grace of God.

Psalm 139:14 I will praise thee: for I am fearfully and wonderfully made: marvelous are thy works, and that my soul knoweth right well.

A BLESSED YOU

Consecrated and focused on serving and pleasing God you are a true example of the lovingkindness of God. Your desire to remain steadfast and faithful despite the storms of life is a testament of how good God has been in your life. Truly for the blessed person the joy of the Lord is their strength.

A blessed you stands assured that God will supply their needs according to His riches in glory. They stand firmly on the Word of God and refuse to take down no matter come what may. Doubt and fear have no place because in Christ Jesus all of their hope is placed.

The blessed you is a well of joy and inspiration that springs forth touching and blessing everyone you meet. On your job you are a light, a source of strength and stability. In your homes, you are that rock portraying God's enduring love, and in your neighborhood, you are a symbol of God's holy righteousness.

St. Matthew 4:8 Blessed are the pure in heart: for they will see God.

A HAPPY YOU

Are you happy? Are you living your best life? If the answer is no, then why not? For as good as God has been to you the answer should always be yes. Troubles come and they will go but we cannot let it hinder us from enjoying all that God provides for us each and every day. Don't you know we hold the power of our happiness in our hands. We cannot let our circumstances define who we are or let it predicate our well-being. Life is too short to live it in regret or saying I wish I could have or should have.

What is that favorite ice cream you like? Where is that place that you have always dreamt of seeing? What doth hinder you? Life is too short for excuses. Life is a gift worth living and each day is a blessing to be counted.

Do you know what makes you happy?

So, what are you going to do about it?

Live your dreams, don't dream your life.

THE POWERFUL ME

With all your getting get understanding and wisdom. Fill yourself with the wisdom of the Word that you may apply it to whatever facet in your life. Enrich yourself with knowledge and your eyes will open many doors and the wonders of the world. Accompany yourself with blessed people and you will the life as a child of the King blessed and favored of God.

The skies are the limit for those who dare to live, and with no holds barred the best is yet to come.

Find strength in the love of family and friends.

Seek encouragement from those who bless your presence.

Search for wisdom from those who know the way.

Embrace the time and enjoy the life you have been given.

Be positive and productive.

THE HEALTHY YOU (PHYSICALLY)

A major part of the 'Inspired You' starts with a healthy body. Taking good care of oneself so that we can be the version of ourselves can be the most rewarding thing we can do. As we age it becomes paramount that we treat our bodies with the utmost care. Meaning a change in diets, adequate rest for these bodies, and limiting our stress levels. And to those taking medicine have at it. Time out for taking our bodies for granted. Our bodies should be treated like temples of God and just doing any old things will not do.

As we grow older our bodies change and we need to adjust our care for it. We might not be able to run up and down the stairs like we use to or eat anything that our hearts or our stomach desire, but we can make sure that we are in reasonable shape or condition. If that means baked instead of fried, have it. If it means eating before 7:00 and no more midnight snacks, then so be it. What matters is a healthy you with a reasonable portion of your health and strength.

Just a thought to add days to your life and lessen those creeping pounds. Remember we are no good to anyone else if we are no good to ourselves.

- See your doctors regularly
- Find time to exercise even if it is to stretch
- Make sure you get proper rest

THE HEALTHY YOU (MENTALLY)

The "Inspired You" focuses on healthy thoughts. Thoughts that are positive and productive. Thoughts that work to improve you. Thoughts that inspire others around you to be the best that they can be.

It is our mental state of mind that we need to protect and nourish like never before. Our self-esteem is constantly bombarded and attacked throughout the course of the day. We are tested and tried time and time again, zapping away our virtue and bringing us down. But we have the tools to endure. We can face each obstacle with victorious thinking by trusting God and letting Him lead and guide our paths.

The healthy you seek those who can add to their better state of mind. They avoid stressful people, places, and things. They enjoy and appreciate all that life has to give them.

* Read a book

* Take a walk

* Pray and meditate

* Take a nap when time permits

Philippians 4:8 Finally brethren, whatsoever things are true, whatsoever things are honest, whatsoever things are just, whatsoever things are pure, whatsoever things are lovely, whatsoever things are of good report: if there be any virtue and if there be any praise, think on these things.

THE HEALTHY YOU(SPIRITUALLY)

The healthy inspired you would be incomplete without a healthy spiritual you. As Christ centered beings our most humble desire is that we draw closer to God. He is the center of our joy, our strength, and our peace. Our souls are at rest when we seek His guidance and wisdom.

The Inspired You by all means necessary seeks a stronger relationship with God. We want to be able to know His will in our lives and that can only occur by studying His Word daily and through a consistently praying and fasting. The healthy spiritual you are a beacon of light and hope. Your life is a testament of the goodness of the Lord and others are drawn to you.

Isaiah 55:8 Seek the Lord while He may be found, call upon him while He is near.

Matt 6:33 But seek ye first the kingdom of God and his righteousness and all these things shall be added unto you.

I AM BLESSED

AND THERE IS NOTHING YOU
CAN DO ABOUT IT

THE QUIET YOU

Silence is golden. It brings serenity and it restores peace. All day long we are taking things into our spirit as well as releasing them. Some good and some bad. So why not take time to shut things down. Time to clear your thoughts. Time to look back on the things that was and look forward to the things that can be.

Quiet time gives you time to process and set in order the affairs of the heart. It gives you time to settle your spirit so that you can dedicate the opportunity to hear from the Lord. It also helps you appreciate the life you have lived and see the beauty that is all around you.

1 Thessalonians 4:11 And that you study to be quiet, and to do your own business, and to work with your own hands, as we commanded you.

AN EDUCATED YOU

An educated you is an empowered you. Knowledge and wisdom go hand in hand when used properly. Unlock the possibilities of life by opening your understanding to the depths that the world has to offer. Broaden your horizon and seek the wonders of life by furthering your education. An educated you is a knowledgeable person full of bright ideas and concepts that can help change and mold the world we live in. An educated you is a resource that can help brighten the paths of others.

An educated you is always hungry for more knowledge knowing there is always something better ahead. They realize that education continues far passed the classroom walls. It is gained through the experiences of life and can be used to be a blessing to others.

Education is the framework that takes us to higher levels of life spiritually and naturally. As children of God, we seek to draw closer to God by staying in His Word and applying it to our lives. The more we know of God the stronger in the faith we become. The more we learn of God the more we appreciate.

Philippians 3:10 That I may know him, and the power of his resurrection and the fellowship of his sufferings, being made conformable unto his death.

THE ACTIVE YOU

The active you is a productive you. The active you is a healthy you. The active exudes energy and is a positive force that is a sure enough force of nature. When both the mind and body are in motion there becomes no place or time for complacency or negativity. The active you yearn for the best that life has to offer and will not stop until that goal is achieved. The active you is determined not to be locked down or held down by 'I can't' or 'I shouldn't'. They seize the moment and press forward come what may.

The active you have an industrious spirit and is willing to put their hand to the plow whenever and wherever is necessary. The active you look forward with vision and hope for today's dream is tomorrow's future.

Live your dream. Don't dream your life.

Proverbs 13:4 the soul of the sluggard desireth, and hath nothing but the soul of the diligent shall be made fat.

A VALUED YOU

Perhaps it all starts with how we value ourselves. Or even how we see ourselves. Yes, it is true that we value the opinions of others but even that has its limits. Do they see us for who we are or for what they want to see us? Does it really matter? We need to see ourselves as blessed and favored children of the King of Glory. We are beautifully unique wonders of the living God.

As we grow older and hopefully wiser, we develop into the person God has designed us to be. We live, we love, we learn. Day by day through life's twisted journey we blossom into the jewel that we are today. Through heartache and pain, sunshine and rain we are ever being molded and perfected.

You see no one knows the total you but God. And He has made us to be magnificent treasures. And so, it is some of us through the fire, some of us through the rain but to His glory we have made it through. We are walking, breathing marvels within ourselves.

Cherish the moment, live your life, and enjoy who you are.

Ecclesiastes 3:11 He hath made everything beautiful in his time: also, he hath set the world in their heart, so that no man can find out the work that God Maketh from the beginning to the end.

AN INNOVATIVE YOU

We were created to do great and marvelous things. We have distinctive gifts that can enlighten and inspire. We have talents that help and strengthen those around us. The innovative you is a difference maker. It is through your time, talent, and treasure many are blessed.

An innovative you is full of thoughts and ideas, ways and means to make better the lives of those around you. They are not afraid to be wrong because through their steadfastness and diligence success is around the corner.

An innovative you is a trendsetter, the first of their kind awaiting their turn for success. Exuding excitement others are drawn to them. They move mountains with their ingenuity and build bridges with their passion

BE A PART OF SOMETHING GREATER

A truth that shows we can become who we keep in our company. We draw from those around us whether it be positive or negative. Their influence can have a lasting impression. If you want to bake a cake surround yourself with those who have made cakes. If you want to start a business surround yourself with successful business owners. If you want to be happy surround yourself with happy people. Get my drift? Blessed people surround themselves with blessed people, don't they?

We are molded and shaped by the ones we keep company with. So why not keep company with the positive difference makers those reaching for higher heights and deeper depths in Christ Jesus. Those seeking to be a blessing to those in need.

As we look ahead to greater things in life. Live your life with purpose. Find joy and meaning in the things you do. Be grateful for all that you have, taking nothing for granted.

PERSON OF CHARACTER

We are people of many layers abounding in the grace of God. Through time we have grown and become better versions of our former selves. Though the process can be arduous at times we find the prize is worth the journey. For we have become men and women of extraordinary character. Our lives exemplary of children of God. Full of integrity, we live to be pleasing to the will of God.

Ever standing on His promises we yet remain prayerful that we can remain steadfast in the service of the Lord. As children of grace our hope lies in our constant trust in the Word. Whether hell or high water we remain determined to seek the face of God therefore taking in the fruits of His spirit.

As persons of exemplary character, we become pillars of our communities as well as our homes. Our lives attract conspicuously as well as inconspicuously. Through the lives we live a path to Christ must and should be seen through us.

Galatians 5:22 But the fruit of the Spirit is love, joy, peace, longsuffering, gentleness, gentleness, goodness, faith

23 Meekness, temperance, against such there is no law.

ACKNOWLEDGEMENTS

To God be the glory for the path that he has taken me to get to this juncture in my life. Things have come and things have gone but it is through the wisdom of God's Word that these words of inspiration have been conceived. We are praying for higher heights and deeper depths i9n our future endeavors.

I want to show appreciation and thanks for the support from my family. Thanks for encouraging words from my wife Sandy. As well as understanding and backing from my children.

I want to say love you Mom Brenda Whittington. Keep being you.

Special acknowledgement to my other Mom, Malverine Davis. Thanks for the support. Love you. Mean it.

Special thanks to my parents in the gospel Bishop William A. Thomas and Evangelist Rosa Lee Thomas. Much appreciation for the teaching of the Word and your leadership this is helping to mold and make in this journey. Thank you for your prayers.

God bless. Stay strong. Stay encouraged.

Made in the USA
Middletown, DE
11 September 2024

60136155R00029